DISCOVER LAND

Peak District

Photographs Simon Kirwan

Text Jerome Monahan

MYRIAD
LONDON

The North Peaks

Most of the North Peak is taken up with a vast area of moorland crossed by a single main road, the A57. It follows the course of a Roman road, running up the central Ladybower and Woodlands valleys and joining Glossop in the west and Sheffield in the east. This is an untamed landscape dominated by peat bogs and occasional gritstone outcrops on the "edges". Only the hardiest of walkers venture out onto the moors proper where the bogs are formidable and the going is distinctly heavy. This is the true "dark peak", dominated by brooding peat moorlands such as Baslow and Kinder Scout, above – the site of one of the most famous acts of civil disobedience in modern times.

But the North Peak does not lack evidence of human influence and settlement. At Peveril Castle (above right) today's ruins can only hint at the imposing presence it must have exerted over the locality – a reminder of the new status quo following the Norman victory at Hastings.

Peveril Castle

Peveril Castle was built in 1080 by William Peverel, possibly the illegitimate son of William the Conquerer and one of his most trusted allies. It defended the royal hunting grounds in the area and also the local lead-mining industry. The castle saw a succession of visits by kings and queens but in the late 14th century it was granted to John of Gaunt, in exchange for the earldom of Richmond, and Peveril then became part of the Duchy of Lancaster. In Tudor times it was thought to be too uncomfortable for royal residence and it went into decline. The keep, however, was maintained as a courthouse. Peveril is at the heart of the Peak District, overlooking Castleton. It offers the visitor breathtaking views over the surrounding countryside, towards Mam Tor (above) and north over the fields around Castleton towards Lose Hill.

Ladybower Reservoir

The Ladybower is one of three reservoirs constructed in the Upper Derwent Valley to supply water to Sheffield, Derby, Nottingham and Leicester; the others are Howden and the Derwent. It was built between 1935 and 1943 and contains more than 6000m gallons of water. There were casualties – namely the villages of Derwent and Ashopton. Much of the stone of Derwent's houses went to reinforce the dam, and Ashopton's site provides the foundations for the viaduct that carries the A57 over the reservoir.

The three stretches of placid water have gone down in history as the site of the practice runs of the Dambusters before their daring wartime raid on the Möhne, Sorpe and Eder dams in the Ruhr. It was here that 617 Squadron flew practice sorties before their successful mission in 1943. The dam's association with this famous exploit continues to be a tourist draw and it is possible to take a helicopter ride along the training route.

The village of Castleton

The pretty little village of Castleton nestles at the foot of the looming Mam Tor and guards the entrance to Winnats Pass and the dramatic Speedwell Cavern. It is a medieval village and is centred on its church, St Edmund's, and main square. The settlement was laid out on a grid pattern towards the end of the 12th century.

St Edmund's was a victim of Victorian restoration, but its Norman arch across the nave survives. Built between 1190-1250, it is considered to be one of the finest churches in the region. Other signs of the Norman era still remain – across the road by the Bull's Head Inn you can see a section of the Town Ditch, a defensive earthwork built around the village.

Around Castleton's square are some fine old houses and cottages, including a youth hostel, a Peak District National Park visitor centre, the George Inn and several houses which offer teas and/or bed-and-breakfast. On the main road there are rows of shops, but most of them sell only Blue John (a local variety of fluorspar with a fine colouring), jewellery made from this or souvenirs. One shop here houses the Ollerenshaw Collection, which contains a range of fine specimens of Blue John.

Castleton environs

The area around Castleton has been described as "the most educational of all landscapes". The village is situated at the top of the Hope Valley, on the border of the Dark and White Peak areas of the national park. The northern slopes of the valley are composed of shale and gritstone rocks, typical of the Dark Peak. The southern slopes rise to form a limestone plateau associated with the White Peak. The presence of Peveril Castle, the gorges and the limestone caves and caverns have also added to the area's attractions making it a major tourist hub, especially in the summer. And where there are tourists there is a need for tea and cakes and picturesque buildings in which to consume them. One of the most well-known of these in Castleton is the Three Roofs Café, located opposite the main car park. The beautiful Odin Sitch (right) runs through the village, bordered by a drystone wall. The ancient Odin mine was located at the foot of Mam Tor from where silver and lead was extracted.

Lose Hill Pike

A highly enjoyable, though strenuous, 6.5 mile (10km) walk starts in Castleton, takes the rambler across the Hope Valley to the gradually swelling shape of Lose Hill, rising to 1560ft (476m) above sea level. At the summit a stone way-marker (below) surmounted by an engraved brass plate can be seen. It carries information about all the surrounding scenery.

Lose Hill was made famous by George Herbert Bridges Ward (1876-1957) the founder of the Sheffield Clarion Ramblers. One of the great campaigners for access to the countryside, he was passionate about the history, place-names and folklore of the Peak District. In May 1945 the Sheffield ramblers bought Lose Hill Pike, together with 54 surrounding acres, and presented the land to the National Trust in appreciation of the work of GHB Ward and his wife Fannie. To quote from the commemorative plaque, "Much of our freedom on these Derbyshire moors & valleys is due to his untiring efforts".

The Shivering Mountain

Mam Tor (above right) dominates the Hope Valley. At 1700ft (518m) its softly undulating shape gave rise to the name Mam Tor – the "mother mountain". But its other nickname is "the Shivering Mountain", testament to the instability of the sedimentary rocks from which it is formed. The sandstone and shale combination is highly friable causing the slopes to crumble.

One of the most spectacular recent rockfalls occurred in 1979, effectively sealing the fate of the old route of the A625, trans-Pennine road (above), forcing it to take its current course over Winnats Pass.

The Pennine Way *(right)*

It is arguably the most famous of all England and Wales' national trails. The Pennine Way is a 268 mile (430km) path that starts in the Peak District National Park, joins the Pennine ridge, passes through the Yorkshire Dales, continues up into Northumberland, traverses the Cheviots and eventually ends in the Scottish Borders. It is described as a "grand traverse of the backbone of England" and takes a fit walker about 16 days.

The photograph (right) is of the path that confronts walkers as they set out from Edale and prepare to tackle the first major incline up Kinder.

The Last Chance Saloon

The Nag's Head is the last refreshment stop for walkers stepping out on the Pennine Way from Edale – a place where heavy boots and Labradors are welcome, both still free of the heavy peat that will soon be weighing on feet and paws alike.

The little village of Edale was really put on the map after the construction of a railway link between Manchester and Sheffield. Previously the valley had been reserved for royal hunting and sheep farming. In the 20th century its name became inextricably linked to the right of access campaign culminating in the mass trespass on Kinder Scout in 1932.

Mam Tor *(above and below)*

History does not record when the rock fall that created the spectacular eastern exposed face of Mam Tor occurred, but it was likely to have been the moment when the peak earned its reputation as the "shivering mountain". The area below the face is unstable and when rainfall has been heavy the shale is undermined and crumbles, causing sections of the strata to slip down into the valley. The trig point marked by a cemented stone cairn (below) on the summit of the hill is placed on top of a tumulus which probably dates from the Bronze Age; a bronze axehead was one of the finds from the site. The Iron Age fort is still easily made out. The ramparts are obvious and there are clear remains of two gateways on the paths leading from Mam Nick and from Hollins Cross. Hut circles have been found within the defences. These plus numerous pottery finds suggest this was a village rather than an occasionally garrisoned fortification.

As well as the spectacular views, Mam Tor is a local centre for hang-gliding, with enthusiasts taking advantage of the winds that continuously buffet this exposed spot.

Doctor's Gate (above)

An old road brings walkers to Doctor's Gate – the name derived from a 16th-century Glossop medical man who travelled this route. It is hard to imagine that this area, now dotted with walkers in all but the most savage weather, was out of bounds for more than a century, thanks to an Act of Enclosure in 1836. That we can now wander this stunning spot – and Kinder Scout, a 15-mile (24km) plateau of wind and ice-shattered boulders, peat bogs and groughs – is thanks in large part to 400 walkers and their mass trespass of April 24 1932. The event was specifically mentioned in the 1945 Dower Report that led to the creation of the UK's national parks.

Kinder Downfall (right)

Kinder Scout is thought to derive its name from *kyndwr scut*, the Anglo-Saxon for "water over the edge". Nowhere is this more appropriate than at Kinder Downfall, where most of the plateau's water gathers to drop over 98ft (30m). In the winter the flow can freeze, creating a ribbon of refracting silver against the dark slopes of the Kinder Downfall amphitheatre. Writing in 1908, JB Firth said of Kinder Scout: "...great boulders stand up on the summit, jagging the skyline, and at intervals along the steep precipitous sides there are clefts from top to bottom, some so deep as to resemble chasms with bare sides and courses for torrents in their stony beds..."

The Mass Trespass

Firth knew Kinder at a time when the place was off limits to all but the invited guests of local landowners. All was to begin to change with the mass trespass of 1932 when 400 men, women and children, organised by the British Workers' Sports Federation, set out onto Kinder from Hayfield. This was just one among many organised trespasses in the 1930s but it became the most celebrated. In 1982 a plaque was unveiled in Bowden Bridge Quarry, near Hayfield, where the 400 originally gathered.

The trespass was led by Benny Rothman (1911-2002) who was arrested along with five others and charged with riotous assembly. Rothman was sent to prison for five months; within weeks, more than 10,000 people demonstrated their support on Kinder Scout. This action led to the establishment of the Ramblers Association and, after the war, to the setting up of national parks, starting with the Peak District in 1951.

Kinder Reservoir and Kinder Bank

The river Kinder's flow now contributes to the expanse of water that is Kinder Reservoir, a beautiful backdrop no doubt for the fortunate residents of Upper House (seen in the photograph of Kinder Bank, right). Construction of the Kinder Reservoir was completed in 1911. Built from local stone and clay, the reservoir was created to supply nearby Stockport. In order to transport the building materials to this remote spot, a special railway spur was created, but the two-mile track and the "tin town" of workers' shacks that sprang up just north of Bowden Bridge have long since vanished.

Route to the Top

The William Clough is the name of the path up the side of Kinder Reservoir to the high ground above. This was the route taken by the 1932 Kinder Scout trespassers. It was from here that the walkers mounted their assault on the slopes of Sandy Heys, intending to reach the plateau above. They were met by about 20 gamekeepers and some brief struggles broke out. A victory celebration was held near Ashop Head and the group then made their way back into Hayfield where the police arrested six people. The actions of the "mass trespassers" paved the way for the creation of Britain's national parks.

Hayfield *(above and below)*

In the Domesday Book it was referred to as "Hedfeld". Its main river is the Sett, which played a key role in Hayfield's industrial past. It is hard to believe, wandering this picturesque place, that it was once a home to wool and cotton manufacture, paper-making and textile printing. Before the flow of the river was controlled by the development of the Kinder Reservoir, it had also been a curse, flooding the village on a number of occasions and even disinterring corpses from the graveyard.

For the visitor, Hayfield is the gateway to the west side of Kinder and there are beautiful walks along the Sett valley and to the neighbouring village of Little Hayfield.

Waterfall, William Clough *(right)*

The descent of William Clough takes walkers past a number of delightful small waterfalls and pools which occur along the way.

The Central Peaks

The central part of the Peak District National Park is often described as the "White Peak", due to the prominence of limestone deposited in the Carboniferous period about 350 million years ago. It was laid down before the development of the gritstone moors and gives an altogether gentler landscape. Its fields and woods are linked by over 26,000 miles of drystone walls. It is an area of important settlement and history – not least at Eyam, where the population made perhaps one of the most selfless acts in recent history to safeguard their neighbouring villages from death and disease.

Buxton – The Crescent

The success of Buxton as an elegant spa town was brought about by the 5th Duke of Devonshire, who was responsible for the building of the fashionable Crescent (above) around the main spring and the Great Stables (1789), later to become part of the Devonshire Royal Hospital and now part of the University of Derby.

Pavilion Gardens

Buxton entered a period of decline in the 1970s and 80s but its fortunes are on the ascendancy again, thanks in part to the town's annual music festival, centred on the Edwardian Opera House, which is located in 25 acres of ornamental gardens at the heart of the town. The gardens also accommodate ornamental waters, a pavilion and concert hall, a theatre and reading rooms.

The hothouse is home to numerous tropical and sub-tropical plants, providing a refuge from the winter cold. The neighbouring Octagon was originally a concert hall designed by Robert Rippon Duke.

Monsal Head Viaduct

The Monsal Trail follows the course of the old Midland Railway through the very heart of the Peak District. The building of the line was opposed by the Dukes of Devonshire and Rutland, coming too close for comfort to their estates. Devonshire refused it access entirely to the grounds of Chatsworth Park; his neighbour, Rutland, struck a deal whereby the railway was hidden from Haddon Hall thanks to the construction of a tunnel. Today, the viaduct has blended into the scenery and would be missed were it to vanish. The views it provides up the Monsal valley are some of the most spectacular in the national park.

Miller's Dale

The glory days of Miller's Dale are associated with the local railway junction where passengers for Buxton made their connections between London and Manchester on the old Midland Railway. In 1964 the station and line closed leaving the spot to sink into obscurity, except that it is now an ideal starting point for walkers eager to explore the local limestone scenery. The hamlet is still dominated by the massive railway viaducts across the Wye valley (right).

Great Rocks Dale Quarry *(above)*

Large-scale quarrying began in the Buxton area in the late 19th century. This industrial activity has had a dramatic effect on the landscape of the nearby dales.

Monsal Dale *(right)*

The river Wye rises in the millstone plateau west of Buxton, passing through some spectacular countryside before joining the river Derwent at Rowsley. Among the several Dales it crosses is Monsal Dale. There are a number of weirs along the river's length which add to the delights on offer to walkers following the nine-mile Monsal Trail. It runs from the Coombs Road viaduct, about a mile south of Bakewell to Blackwell Mill junction, three miles or so from Buxton.

Ashford-in-the-Water

The presence of Ashford in the Domesday Book underlines its ancient origins. Its beauty is enhanced by the river Wye, its main attraction being the "sheep wash" bridge where, until recently, sheep were washed prior to shearing. The lambs would be placed in the stone-walled pen on one side of the river, and the mothers would be thrown in at the other side. Their lambs' bleats would force them to swim across the river giving their coats a thorough soaking.

In the 19th century Ashford was famous for the black marble so beloved by the Victorians for fireplaces, vases and jewellery. Many of the stone cottages in the village served as workshops for its production before the marble works were established by a Bakewell man, Henry Watson, in 1748.

Eyam

Eyam is a wonderfully preserved Peak village. It is the famous "plague village", which went into voluntary quarantine when the plague arrived from London in 1665. Above the village lies Eyam Moor which is a fine area for walking, with good views across the Derwent Valley and many Bronze Age remains and monuments.

When the plague struck Eyam in 1665, the rector, the Rev William Mompesson, and Thomas Stanley persuaded the entire community to place itself in quarantine and thus managed to stop it spreading to the surrounding area. Two years later 259 villagers were dead; many of the houses bear plaques commemorating those who succumbed to the disease.

Once the plague struck, the Rev William Mompesson closed St Lawrence (below) and services were held in Cucklett Delph, a small valley nearby. In August every year a thanksgiving service is held at Cucklett to mark

their sacrifice. The fenced stone (above) was one of the places where supplies were left by people from neighbouring villages during Eyam's period of quarantine.

Many of Eyam's houses have plaques giving details of their history and the part their inhabitants played in the plague saga. On the main street lies Eyam Hall (left) built in 1676 but in a style which was already out of fashion, so it looks like an early Jacobean mansion. It is the home of the Wright family who built it and have lived there ever since, and it is open to visitors in the summer months.

Tideswell

Tideswell, another of the lovely market towns of the Peak District, is situated about nine miles east of Buxton, within the national park. It is one of the most ancient settlements in the central Peak District. It was the site of the "Great Courts" of the Royal Forest of the Peak in the time of Edward I. The name is thought to have been inspired by a local resident who went under the name of "Tidde".

The village was a centre for the lead-mining industry from medieval times to the 19th century. It also had a weekly market during the same period but the Market Place is now the only remnant of that tradition.

The Cathedral of the Peaks (right)

Tideswell's principal attraction all year round is the 14th-century church of St John the Baptist. Known locally as "The Cathedral of the Peaks", it is a tribute to the strength of the local economy in the Middle Ages.

The church has a beautiful high nave and a number of outstanding wooden carvings by the Hunstone family, a famous woodcarving family. Local poet William Newton, "the minstrel of the Peaks" is buried here.

One of Tideswell's main annual summer attractions is the carnival and well-dressing ceremony. This is a focus for the whole community and draws visitors from far and wide.

Carl Wark from Over Owler Tor *(above)*

The landscape is surreal, almost lunar on Higger Tor, where rounded rocks perch delicately one on top of another as if placed there by human hand. The landscape beyond is boggy and hard-going though home to many small birds, mammals and many varieties of water-loving wild plant.

Carl Wark is a remarkable escarpment hill fort. Over 984ft (300m) high, it makes use of natural sheer cliffs on three sides to provide an easily defended position. This is a hill fort the origins of which are still contested – it could date from either the Iron or Dark Ages. Bronze Age artefacts are also close by and show a long general occupation of the area.

Carl Wark appears to occupy a significant position and may well have figured in the defence of their land by the Brigantes, a local tribe at the time of the Roman invasion of Britain.

Two Views of Over Owler Tor *(left and above)*

Walkers describe this landscape as "rounded". Over Owler Tor lies about 1246ft (380m) above sea level and gives spectacular views of the surrounding landscape. Here, the sights to the north-west include the town of Hathersage and the river Derwent. Parts of the Hope Valley near Hathersage are thought to have been the inspiration for sections of *Jane Eyre*. Charlotte Bronte was a friend of Ellen Nussey, whose brother was the vicar of Hathersage and she was their visitor in 1845.

Directly east of Over Owler Tor is a flattened plateau of rocks and heather. It is a lonely spot now, but evidence of earlier settlement and use abounds including signs of an ancient field system and quarries. Rocks here are etched and eroded by wind and rain to appear almost hand-made. The Peaks stand at a natural cross-roads marking the meeting place of highland and lowland creating a fascinating overlap of both flora and fauna.

The East Peaks

This is an area of richly contrasting scenery encompassing rolling farmland, remote moors and "edges" – those spectacular steep escarpments that typify the region and hint at the powerful forces that have governed its geology over the millennia. It is also a landscape of river scenery and is crossed by the Derwent and the Wye. The Derwent passes through and near towns picturesque now, Cromford and Matlock, but once the cradle of this nation's burgeoning commercial strength, playing a pivotal role in the Industrial Revolution.

Bakewell Bridge

Little survives of medieval Bakewell today except the town's early 14th-century bridge with its row of five typically Gothic arches. The bridge is still in use and is thought to be one of the oldest in Britain. It is a reminder of the town's origins as a key route over the river Wye for the wool drovers and merchants.

The Weir

It is possible for walkers to pause and admire the weir just downriver from Bakewell's medieval bridge as they explore the riverside route through the town. Here the "fall" created by the weir is gentle, its sound a calming antidote to the traffic of the town, swelled these days by a stream of visitors. In summer, with bankside trees masking the landscape beyond, it is easy to imagine oneself on an entirely rural section of the river Wye, instead of just a few hundred paces from the hurly-burly of Bakewell – the East Peak's unofficial "capital".

Lead Mines and Quarries

In the 17th and 18th centuries fortunes were made by those in the East Peaks with control of lead-mining. But in the 19th century the industry went into decline, as the shafts went deeper and deeper, became prone to flooding and finally lost out to more easily mined Australian lead. The landscape around Wirksworth and Middleton still bears the scars. Even more noticeable are the limestone quarries, sunk into the local hills and mountains in response to the needs of agriculture and industry. Both towns suffered significant dust and noise pollution, but with the closure of the quarries and concerted action to improve the environment, the area is enjoying a rebirth as a popular tourist destination. Middleton Top now boasts a visitors' centre celebrating the area's industrial heritage.

Bakewell Tarts

While Bakewell has one of the oldest markets in the area, dating from at least 1300, one item for sale today has more recent origins. The famous "Bakewell pudding" (often called "Bakewell tart" in error) was first created in 1860 when a cook employed by a Mrs Greaves at the Rutland Arms Hotel confused her pie-making instructions. Mrs Greaves left the recipe in her will. Today Bakewell tarts feature prominently on signs outside the town's many bakeries.

Chatsworth

Often referred to as "the Palace of the Peak", the present house at Chatsworth is largely the creation of the first Duke of Devonshire who, between 1686 and 1707, re-modelled the original house – built by the formidable Bess of Hardwick and her second husband William Cavendish – and turned it into a fabulous Palladian mansion. In the years between 1569 and 1584 Mary Queen of Scots was held prisoner at Chatsworth and some rooms in the house are still known as the Queen of Scots apartments. Chatsworth is a treasure house of works of art and antiques; its superb parkland setting was achieved by the 18th century gardener Lancelot "Capability" Brown who swept away the formal gardens and created today's open, natural-looking landscape.

The best view of the main facade of the house is from the banks of the river Derwent or from the old bridge. To the front of the house is the Canal Pond with its famous gravity-fed Emperor Fountain powered directly from the Emperor Lake 400ft (121m) above the Canal Pond. Every day at 2pm the fountain reaches a height of 200ft (60m), although it is capable of reaching twice this height.

The gardens

The magnificent grounds at Chatsworth are the work of two landscape gardeners of genius: Capability Brown and Joseph Paxton. Brown established the natural setting for the house, which included moving the ancient village of Edensor, whilst Paxton enthused his friend the sixth Duke with his passion for gardening and added greenhouses, water features and fountains. The refurbished Orangery which originally housed tender plants and sculpture, is now a shop.

The grand Stable Block at Chatsworth was designed by the architect James Paine who also built the bridge over the Derwent.

Formal gardens

Whilst Capability Brown created the parkland setting of Chatsworth, it was Joseph Paxton who designed the gardens close to the house incorporating existing features, such as the Seahorse Fountain and the Cascade. He built an amazing iron-framed conservatory at Chatsworth between 1836-41. This giant structure, the largest glass building in the world at the time, was demolished in 1920. One of the most popular garden features at Chatsworth is the Cascade (right). To the west of the house, the Cascade is a set of 24 stone steps over which water flows from a set of fountains down a vertical drop of 200 feet.

Riber Castle and Matlock Bath

The development of Matlock Bath as a major spa is due to the entrepreneurial flair of John Smedley (1803-1872). He developed the town's potential as a "hydro" to rival similar British and continental towns where ailing Victorians would come to "take the waters"; the photograph (below right) of Matlock Spa, taken high above the Derwent, shows the Pump Room and the Matlock Pavilion, built in 1910.

Smedley constructed Riber Castle (below) for himself. Perched on a hill dominating the town, the house boasted electricity and gas at a time when such conveniences were still highly exotic. In recent years its fortunes have been chequered – current plans include conversion into luxury flats.

Matlock: the County Town

Matlock and its near neighbour Matlock Bath lie just outside the Peak District National Park. Matlock is an important centre and Derbyshire's county town. The Romans may have mined lead here but the town was relatively unimportant until the early 19th century when it developed rapidly as a spa, hastened by the construction of the Midland Railway. In the centre of the photograph (right) is the vast hydro, built by John Smedley in 1853. It functioned as a spa until the 1950s. Today, it is home to the county offices and the Derbyshire Dales Borough Council. Here we see Matlock photographed from the Heights of Abraham. Matlock Bath, a few miles south along the river Derwent, is still a prominent tourist resort.

Cromford

The history of Cromford is intertwined with that of the entrepreneur and early industrial magnate Richard Arkwright (1732-1792). He financed the creation of a spinning frame powered by a water wheel and set up a factory in 1771 in Cromford near the Derwent. The machinery became known as a "water frame". The town's fortunes were further underpinned by the development of canal transport. Cromford Canal opened in 1793, running 15 miles to Langley Mill where it linked with the Erewash Canal. It vastly improved access to the markets of Liverpool and Nottingham. Cotton fibres, textiles, limestone and lead were all transported on barges. Shown in the picture below is Cromford Mill's factory-side canal spur and covered loading quay.

The Heights of Abraham

Matlock and Matlock Bath have an Alpine feel, boosted by the presence of a hard-working cable car, carrying visitors up the 450ft (137m) incline to the Heights of Abraham. The name derives from the site of General Wolfe's victory and death at Quebec in 1759; it was chosen by local people because the narrow gorge of the river Derwent was said to resemble that of the St Lawrence river.

Whereas the town of Matlock is fairly open, Matlock Bath lies in a gorge. Mining has played an important part in the development of the area and the Heights of Abraham has two impressive show caves: Grand Masson Cavern and the Great Rutland Cavern-Nestus Mine, where a little of the mining history of the area can be found. "Nestus" was the Roman name for Matlock. From the Heights of Abraham there are views from the Prospect Tower (a stiff climb of 54 steps) from where it is possible to enjoy a fine view of the surrounding countryside.

South and West Peaks

Writing in the 1880s, John Ruskin declared: "It is only in the clefts of it, and the dingles, that the traveller finds his joy", dismissing the millstone plateaux of the Dark Peaks in cavalier fashion. His joy and that of literally thousands of visitors each year was reserved for the steep-sided valleys carved from exposed limestone associated with the White Peaks of the south and central sections of the national park. This is a startling and colourful landscape, replete with history and opportunities to stand and stare in wonder.

The River Dove *(above)*

The Dove rises on the eastern side of Axe Edge and flows almost southwards to the boundary of the Peak. It marks the border between Derbyshire and Staffordshire for the whole of its length. The river is utterly beautiful and has been recognised as a source of the sublime for many centuries. The Dove is also a famous trout-fishing river, long-associated with Izaak Walton. His book *The Compleat Angler*, published in 1653, records his experiences with line and rod when visiting his friend Charles Cotton at Beresford Hall near Hartington.

Tissington Spires *(right)*

The impressive limestone pillars of Tissington Spires are among the most dramatic features of Dovedale. They are a favourite with both walkers and rock-climbers. High on the eastern bank is Reynard's Cave. This massive detached slab was the mouth of a cavern until the roof fell in. Just beyond is the Lion's Head Rock – so-called because it resembles the head of a lion – and Ilam Rock which rises sheer from the edge of the river.

Stones Island, Carsington

Carsington reservoir was opened in 1992 by the Queen. It attracts walkers, bird-watchers and sailing enthusiasts. Close by is Stones Island, a landscaping feature designed by Lewis Knight. Each of the stones relates to the surrounding countryside. There are toe-holds on every pillar allowing children to get some purchase and to enjoy the views.

Carsington village lies nearby. It contains a preaching cross set up by a monk named Betti and the beautiful 12th-century Church of St Margaret on the bottom slopes of Carsington Pastures. The village was a backwater but has been extended since the development of the reservoir.

Macclesfield

This historic market town is situated on the western edge of the Peak District. Macclesfield developed as an industrial centre, first for the manufacture of buttons and then for the production of silk. By the mid 19th century the town was packed with workshops, either making thread or finished silk goods. The handsome town hall (below), which faces the market square, dates from 1823. Its grand classical facade is a sign of Macclesfield's wealth in its heyday. Many of the town's fine buildings had a connection with the silk trade. The Heritage Centre in Park Lane is a former silk mill. It houses a museum telling the story of this once thriving industry.

The Roaches

The Roaches, with Hen Cloud and
Ramshaw Rocks, form a gritstone
escarpment which marks the
south-western edge of the Peak.
These eye-catching rock
formations are a favourite with
climbers. The Finger Stone (right)
at Ramshaw Rocks is one of the
best known features of the area.
The names of some of the cliff
routes known to climbers are
colourful including Saul's Crack,
Valkyrie and the Mangler. Up on
top the landscape is dominated by
weirdly-shaped rocks and there
are spectacular views of
Tittesworth Reservoir and the
town of Leek, in Staffordshire.

Hen Cloud (left)

Hen Cloud is a separate southern extremity of the
Roaches. It rises spectacularly from the surrounding
moor to 1555ft (410m) above sea level. This is the view
north, looking back at the Roaches across the lowland
gap that separates them. Hen Cloud overlooks the
village of Upper Hulme. At the southernmost foot of the
Roaches is a small hut built into the cliff-face and called
Rockhall Cottage. The cottage is now a climbers' hut
and memorial to Don Whillans, the legendary
mountaineer who pioneered many climbing routes in
the area.

Teggs Nose Country Park

Fluffy storm clouds build above the gentle summit to the east of Tegg's Nose (1148ft/350m). Just east of Macclesfield, the surrounding area is a country park from which walkers can appreciate spectacular views including the Jodrell Bank telescope and Bollington. There is a nature trail here that takes visitors past meadows filled in season with mountain pansies and woodland filled with birdsong all year round.

Sheep gate

Teggs Nose Country Park is dotted with a number of imaginative environmental sculptures based on features which can be found in the surrounding Peaks. Here, a drystone wall has been formed into a gateway resembling a sheepfold. The gate is attractive and helps prevent animals straying across the fields.

Windgather Rocks *(above)*

Windgather Rocks owes its poetic name to the Victorians' mania for christening every outcrop and cave they discovered. On the day this photograph was taken the name was particularly appropriate as the open countryside was being lashed by stiff breezes bending the grasses in the fields to the west of the Goyt Forest.

Lamaload Reservoir *(below)*

Situated north of the A54 Buxton to Macclesfield road, the Lamaload Reservoir supplies drinking water to Macclesfield. To the east is the Goyt Valley. The reservoir was completed in 1964 and is approximately 1010ft (308m) above sea level. Fed by the river Dean, the water piles up behind an impressive, tall concrete dam.

Goyt Valley *(above)*

The river Goyt drains off Axe Edge Moor and flows north, feeding both the Fernilee and Errwood reservoirs on the way. This photograph was taken just north of the Fernilee Reservoir looking across the Goyt Valley to the north. The landscape beyond has many miles of open countryside before the next major settlements of Bollington and Whaley Bridge are reached.

Macclesfield Forest

While the name conjures up images of a densely wooded area, in reality this region contains sporadic patches of woodland. This was true even in the past when Macclesfield Forest was home to boar, wolves and even bear and was a royal hunting preserve. Today, the largest mammals are red, roe and fallow deer. The forest is a working area and as the timber is felled and replanted the woodland scenery is always in a state of change.

Ramshaw Outcrops

Ramshaw Rocks boast many wind and rain-etched outcrops, eroded into shapes suggestive of artistic endeavour. None is more dramatic than the Finger Stone which resembles a giant hand pointing an accusing digit heavenward. Its angle, typical of many of the exposed strata here, is due to the tilting of the bedding rock planes at this point. The moorland enclosed by the gritstone edges in this area produces run-off rivulets and streams that feed the waters of Tittesworth Reservoir to the south.

First published in 2010 by Myriad Books Limited,
35 Bishopsthorpe Road London SE26 4PA

Photographs copyright © Simon Kirwan
Text copyright © Jerome Monahan

Designed by Jerry Goldie Graphic Design
Printed in China

www.myriadbooks.com

ISBN 1 84746 347 9
EAN 978 1 84746 347 0